D0955704

FOGTOWN

WRITER
ANDERSEN GABRYCH

ART
BRAD RADER

GRAY TONES
RIVKAH

LETTERS
SEAN KONOT

FOGTOWN

Karen Berger SVP – Executive Editor
Bob Schreck Editor
Brandon Montclare Asst. Editor
Robbin Brosterman Design Director – Books
Louis Prandi Art Director

Special thanks to Mike Humbert and Lee-Roy Lahey

FOGTOWN
VERTIGO CRIME

Published by DC Comics, 1700 Broadway, New York, NY 10019. Printed in Canada. First Printing. DC Comics, a Warner Bros. Entertainment Company.
HC ISBN: 978-1-4012-1384-8 SC ISBN: 978-1-4012-2950-4

NSF-SFICOC-C0001801
This label applies to the text stock

100% Recycled

July, 1953.
Middle of summer and this town's colder'n a witch's tit.
"The Golden Gate."
People might'a come here for gold, but it ain't why they stayed. Or keep flooding in from all over.
Sure as shit it's not for the ballet or them cutesy-pie cable cars, neither. That bullshit's for wives.
It's them three "F's" that make men do just about anything. FAITH, FORTUNE, and FUCKING.
And in this town the line between 'em gets real blurry. Always been a real loose town.
Whatever you want, you can find it here.
Or DIE looking for it.

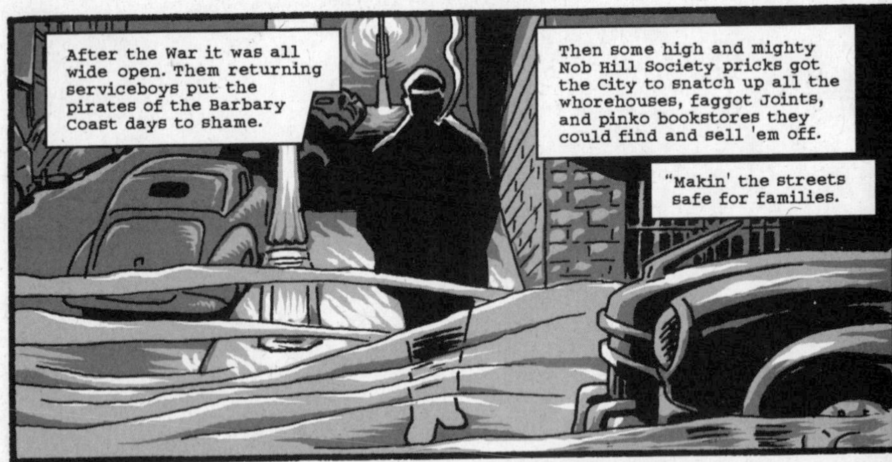
After the War it was all wide open. Them returning serviceboys put the pirates of the Barbary Coast days to shame.
Then some high and mighty Nob Hill Society pricks got the City to snatch up all the whorehouses, faggot Joints, and pinko bookstores they could find and sell 'em off.
"Makin' the streets safe for families.

On the surface things might look pretty, but below--
HIYA, DADDY...
-- they're uglier'n ever.

See, even before the gold diggers this town's always been nothing but missionaries, outcasts, and whores.
...YOU GOT A LIGHT?
And that don't change.

I'M NOT YOUR DADDY.
FLK!
DO YOU WANNA BE?

She's fourteen, if a day.
WELL... IT'S YOUR LAST CHANCE.

UH-HUH. WHY'S THAT?
I'M GONNA BE REAL RICH, REAL SOON.
OH YEAH. SURE.
I AM. YOU'LL SEE.

HERE. THIS'LL KEEP YOU WARM, 'TIL THEN.
BUT, WHO'LL KEEP DADDY WARM?

DON'T
CALL ME--

FORGET
IT, GIRLIE.

YOU AIN'T
MY TYPE.

KEEN.

OH!

YOU SCARED ME.
I WAS JUST GONNA...

WHAT'RE YOU--
--OH GOD--
--NO!

FRANK
GRISSEL
PRIVATE

GET UP.
HNNN... 'RETTA?

WHO ELSE?
NOT LIKE WE'VE HAD A CLIENT IN WEEKS.
HERE. COFFEE.

YOU BEEN FIGHTING, AGAIN.
IT AIN'T HOW IT LOOKS.
YEAH, YEAH. IF I HAD A NICKEL...

C'MERE, LET'S CLEAN YOU UP.
GOD-BLESS IT, LORETTA! YOU'RE MY SECRETARY, NOT MY MOTHER.

DO IT YOURSELF THEN, TOUGH GUY.

YOU DIDN'T COME HOME LAST NIGHT.

KNOCK
KNOCK
KNOCK

HELLO? SENÓR GRISSEL?
WHO'S ASKIN'?
I AM MAGDA.
I AM LOOK FOR MY DAUGHTER. CARMEN.
WELL, MAGDA. SHE AIN'T HERE.
NO. NO. SHE IS GO RUNAWAY.

HERE, PLEASE SIT DOWN.
GRACIAS.
YOU ARE SENÓRA GRISSEL?

NO. I'M JUST THE *SECRETARY.*

I BRING PHOTO.
SEE?
LEMME SEE.

MUY PRETTY, YES?
YEAH. A REAL ANGEL.

FORGET IT.
FRANK!

PERO, NO COMPRENDO...
I HAVE MONEY.

I DON'T CARE.
YOU... NO CARE? BUT... HAVE YOU CHILDREN?

TWENTY-FIVE A DAY, PLUS EXPENSES.

WHOSE NAME'S ON THE DOOR?
THAT'S NOT FAIR.
LIFE AIN'T FAIR.

JEEZ-IT, FRANK, WHAT IS WITH YOU, LATELY?
YOU HAD TO GO BRING UP THE KID.
I DIDN'T--
BUT DON'T YOU EVEN THINK ABOUT HER?

I TOLD YOU--
DO IT! C'MON!
GIMME A REASON TO CHANGE THE LOCKS!

'RETTA...

...I...

SHHH. YOU'RE RIGHT. I SHOULDN'T'VE BROUGHT IT UP.
BETTY'S YOUR BUSINESS.
S'OKAY.

FRANK?
YEAH, BABY?

WHERE DO YOU GO AT NIGHT?

GODDAMN WOMEN AND YOUR FUCKING QUESTIONS!

BEEN AWHILE, GRISSEL. THOUGHT MAYBE YOU WERE OUTTA THE PRIVATE DICK BIZ.
YOU GOT ANYTHING IN A RUNAWAY SPIC HOOKER LATELY, DOC?
WHAT'RE YOU LOOKING FOR?
WHAT'S IT WORTH TO YOU?

THIS DO IT?
THAT IT WILL.

THE CLOSEST WE GOT'S THIS JANE DOE LAST NIGHT. BUT SHE'S A BLONDE.
MEXICANS GOT PEROXIDE, TOO.
OKAY. BUT, GOTTA WARN YA. SHE'S IN ROUGH SHAPE.

THAT'S... NOT HER. BUT... WHAT THE HELL--?

PRETTY SIMPLE. SOME SICK SUCKER CUT OUT HER INSIDES AND TOOK 'EM.
RIGHT ON THE CORNER OF GRANT AND GREEN.
GRANT AND GREEN...
YEAH, PRACTICALLY ON SOME CHURCH DOORSTEP.

I DIDN'T SEE NOTHIN' IN THE PAPERS.
NEWS OF SOME "FRISCO RIPPER" RUNNING AROUND GUTTING PROSTIES ISN'T EXACTLY GOOD FOR THOSE SOARING PROPERTY VALUES.

NOT MUCH STUFF, EVEN FOR A WORKIN' GIRL.
ELIZA GREY, M.D.
PSYCHIATRIST
YUKON - 8282
SENTINEL BUILDING

WHAT'S WITH THE LADY HEAD-SHRINKER?
SOME KINDA LEZZIE-THING?
ELIZA GREY, M.D.
PSYCHIATRIST
YUKON - 8282
SENTINEL BUILDING
YOU WOULDN'T SAY THAT IF YOU SAW HER.
NO, SHE'S DOING ONE OF THEM SEX STUDIES. LIKE THAT... WHAT'S THE-- Y'KNOW, KINSEY REPORT.

DUNNO IT.
YEAH, YEAH, SHE'S BEEN ALL OVER TOWN ASKING ALL THE PROSTIES WHAT THEY DO, WHY THEY DO IT, ABOUT THEIR FAMILIES.
LORDY, I THINK IF ONE'A MY GIRLS--
HEY. NICE ZIPPO.
YOU THINK I COULD--?

SORRY, IT'S ALREADY BEEN TAGGED.
WELL, I BETTER GET GOING, THEN.

SEE YA, LITTLE GIRL.

Blood of the Lamb Ministry.
Dunno why I went there first. My runaway and the dead girl had nothin' to do with each other.
But something in my gut told me to. And it weren't to find the Lord.
SO SAD.
DID YOU KNOW HER?
I'M AFRAID I'M NOT AT LIBERTY TO DISCUSS IT.
MUST'A BEEN A REAL MESS. LOOKS PRETTY CLEAN NOW, PADRE.
MISTAKING LOOKING CLEAN FOR BEING CLEAN IS THE SIN OF PHARISEES, MISTER...?

GRISSEL. I'M A PRIVATE DICK. YOU SEEN THIS GIRL AROUND?

NO, CAN'T SAY AS I HAVE.
AND THIS IS ONE OF THEM MINISTRIES THAT GETS HOOKERS OFF THEIR BACKS, ON THEIR FEET, AND INTO THE ARMS OF JESUS, RIGHT?

CRUDELY PUT. BUT, YES, SOMETHING LIKE THAT.
MIGHTY CHARITABLE, PADRE. MUST BE HARD TO KEEP UP WITH THE RENT 'ROUND HERE, THESE DAYS.
THE CHURCH OWNS THE BUILDING.

AND YOU'RE SURE YOU CAN'T HELP ME OUT.
I'LL LIGHT A CANDLE FOR HER, DETECTIVE. PERHAPS IT WILL HELP TO GUIDE HER HOME.

FATHER FISCHER, I BROUGHT YOU THE HOLY-- OH.
THANK YOU, GREGORY.

HEY, GREG. YOU SEEN THIS GIRL?
I... NO. I DUNNO.

PARDON ME, DETECTIVE--
ISAIAH 1:16, GREGORY.

"YOU ARE STAINED RED WITH SIN, BUT I WILL WASH YOU AS CLEAN AS SNOW. ALTHOUGH YOUR STAINS ARE DEEP RED, THEY WILL BE AS WHITE AS WOOL."

AMEN.

WELL, THANKS FOR YOUR TIME, PADRE. GUESS I'LL SEE WHAT THAT LADY SHRINK'S GOT TO SAY.
NOT DR. GREY?
THAT'S THE ONE. YOU KNOW HER?

WATCH OUT. SHE'S A DANGEROUS WOMAN.
DANGEROUS, HUH?

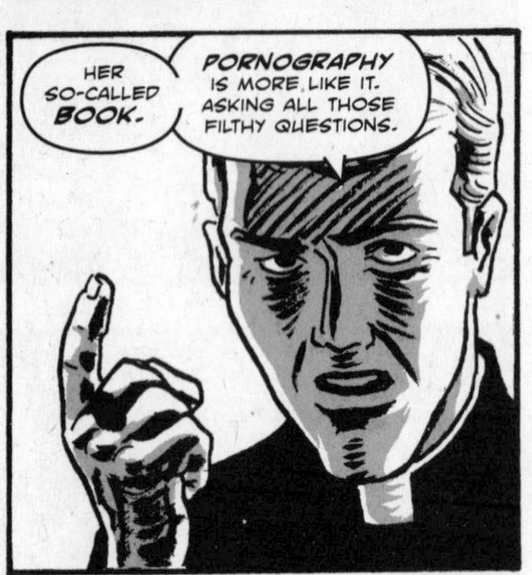
HER SO-CALLED BOOK.
PORNOGRAPHY IS MORE LIKE IT. ASKING ALL THOSE FILTHY QUESTIONS.

HOW ABOUT YOU, GREG? SHE ASK YOU ANY DIRTY QUESTIONS?
PLEASE REFRAIN FROM TRAUMATIZING THE POOR BOY, MR. GRISSEL.

OH, I GOT A HUNCH THE POOR BOY'S HANDLED WORSE.

RIGHT, PADRE?

Nice Caddy. Parked right up to a hydrant.
Somebody's tight with the boys in blue.

Byron "Bone" White. Four-time Golden Gloves Heavyweight champ. drafted in '42. discharged in '44. Section 8. Go figure.

Since then, this 275 pounds of "psycho-logically disturbed colored muscle's been on the payroll for JAMES THORPE, THE 3rd.

A genuine million-aire and leader of them Nob Hill "HOLIER THAN THOUS."
They call him "THE COLONEL." Dunno why.

Bone's nickname comes from when he HITS you...

... it goes STRAIGHT to the bone.

ELIZA GREY, M.D.
CLINICAL PSYCHIATRIST
NOK NOK
C'MON IN. I DON'T BITE.
YOU'RE... DOCTOR GREY?

AND TO WHOM DO I OWE THE PLEASURE...?
I'M A P.I. NAME'S FRANK GRISSEL.

REALLY? LIKE THE MEAT? OR THE ATTITUDE?
HUH?
GRISTLE OR GRIZZLE?
NEITHER. G-R-I-DOUBLE-S-E-L.

PRIVATE
In a flash, her Jade eyes tear me apart, hungrily look at each piece, and put me back together again.

YOU'RE PRACTICALLY A JUNGIAN IDEAL.
PRIVATE
Fucking Head-Shrinkers.

WELL, NOW, I BEEN CALLED A LOTTA THINGS BY DAMES BEFORE, BUT NEVER IDEAL.
HEH.

A "COME-ON" THAT'S BOTH SELF-CONGRATULATORY AND SELF-DEPRECATING? I'M IMPRESSED.
THEM'RE SOME BIG WORDS THERE, DOCTOR.

MY, MY, MY, MR. FRANK GRISSEL, P.I.
IT'S NOT EVERY DAY YOU MEET A TRUE-BLUE CLICHÉ.

AND I SAY THAT AS A DAME...
...AND A DOCTOR.

A CLICHÉ, HUH?
WELL, YOU COME HERE FROM THE MIDWEST--
-- GREEN BAY'S MY BET, FROM THE ACCENT AND THE WALLOON NAME--
-- RUNNING AWAY FROM WHO YOU WERE AND LOOKING FOR WHO YOU ARE. BUT THEN YOU GOT LOST ALONG THE WAY.

MAYBE YOU SHOULD BE THE DETECTIVE.

I ALREADY HAVE A JOB.
RUNNING SOME KINDA KINKY SURVEY, YEAH?
I AM CONDUCTING A SERIOUS SCIENTIFIC STUDY THAT--

YEAH, YEAH, YEAH. ALL I CARE IS, YOU EVER RUN INTO THIS GIRL?
NAME'S CARMEN?

AS I TOLD THE POLICE AND THAT THUG, I HAND OUT MY CARD A LOT. I DON'T HEAR BACK FROM MOST. THERE'S A LOT OF SHAME ASSOCI--
WHAT'S THE SHAME IS THERE'S A LITTLE MAMACITA WHO NEEDS HER BABY SAFE AT HOME.

THAT WAS A RATHER CLUMSY AND INSINCERE APPEAL TO MY MATERNAL INSTINCT.
YOU DON'T CARE ABOUT THAT GIRL OR HER MOTHER.
I DON'T?

NO. YOU'RE AN OVER-THE-HILL DRUNK WHO ONLY CARES ABOUT KILLING THE REGRET OVER EVERY BAD CHOICE YOU'VE EVER MADE.

WAS THERE ANYTHING ELSE, FRANK?

LIQUO

ADLE

INTO THE ALLEY. NOW.
CRASH!

HANDS ON THE WALL!
WHY, GREGGIE-PIE. THAT A KNIFE IN MY SIDE, OR YOU JUST HAPPY TO SEE ME?

NO JOKES!
WHY YOU WANT CARMEN?

YOU'RE A LIAR, GREG.
AND YOU OWE ME FOR A FIFTH OF RYE.

HOW YOU WANNA PAY FOR IT?

DON'T TOUCH ME, KID.
JUST SHOW ME WHERE YOU LAST SAW HER.
WELL, I DIDN'T SEE HER AROUND FOR A MONTH, AND THEN DAY BEFORE YESTERDAY, I SAW HER--

-- AND YOU SWEAR YOU'RE GOING TO TAKE HER STRAIGHT TO HER MOM? RIGHT?
NOWHERE ELSE?
THAT'S RIGHT.

YOU CAN'T TELL ANYONE I TOLD YOU, OKAY? NOT EVEN CARMEN. 'CAUSE IF THEY FOUND OUT--
WHO'S THEY?
Y'KNOW, FATHER FISCHER AND Y'KNOW... THE MINISTRY.
FUCK THEM.

OKAY. DOWN THERE'S A QUEER LITTLE OFFICE.
WHAT WAS CARMEN DOING THERE?
SHE'S HIS FAVORITE.
WHOSE?

I GOTTA GO, IF SHE SEES ME...
YEAH, SCRAM, KID.

The smell hits me like a truck.
Shit and rot and old paper.
It's the smell of...

... DEAD BOOKKEEPERS.

Been that way for a day. Maybe two. His tracks say he's been riding the horse a long time.

Dollars to donuts there's one reason a lifelong junkie O.D.'s--

--He WANTS to.

The dope is clean. Uncut. Fresh off the boat from China.
Looks like this place is bringin' in more than soy sauce and fortune cookies.
Somebody was looking for something. Whatever it was, he died because it was gone.

How the hell do Chinamen read this scratch?
Wait. What's that?

Even if it wasn't in English.
BLACK CAT CAFE
You bet I know a BAR TAB when I see one.
BLACK
CAFE
The Black Cat.
Been in the Tenderloin for twenty years. Not eight blocks from my office. Never been inside.
Not my kinda joint. it ain't the hookers, or the commies; it's the FRUITS.
See, this place fought the City's queer-bar crackdown all the way to the Supreme Court last year. And WON.
So it's still here. THEY'RE still here.
REGRETFULLY THE BLACK CAT IS UNABLE TO SERVE MEMBERS OF THE U.S. MILITARY
But SOMEBODY had to go.

... SAID IT HIMSELF, "MCCARTHYISM IS AMERICANISM WITH ITS SLEEVES ROLLED UP."
WHATTYA EXPECT? HE'S FROM WISCONSIN.
... SO TALLULAH HAD TO SIT HERE FOR THE ENTIRE SHOW.
DEVASTATING.
AND THIS CEASEFIRE IDEA OF EISENHOWER'S, DUNNO **WHAT** THAT'LL MEAN.
... SUDDENLY VOMITED BORING LITTLE BUILDINGS ALL OVER THE RICHMOND...
MEANS WE **LOST,** MAN.
... GOING TO **DENMARK** FOR IT...
... AND NOW THERE'S **CHINESE** EVERYWHERE TAKING OUR **JOBS...**
... PREGNANT AND STILL LUCY AND RICKY ARE IN **DIFFERENT BEDS?**
"... I LOAF AND INVITE MY SOUL..."

HEY!
WHICH OF YOU FREAKS, PHONIES, AND FAGS KNOWS WHERE I CAN FIND A WETBACK WHORE NAMED CARMEN?!

BLACK
CAFE
AND STAY OUT!
BLACK CAT CAFE
LUNCH

I duck behind a car. Watch the door.

And BINGO.

Oh, for Christ...
Who the fuck WANTS to look French?

HOTEL
STRATFORD

Pete Seeger record plays.
The heavy sweet stench of opium and reefer.
Means one thing: BOHEMIANS.

WHAM
I like Bohemians.
They scare easy.

MOVE AWAY FROM THE GIRL AND NO ONE GETS HURT.

C'MON, LITTLE GIRL, YOU'RE COMING WITH ME.
HUHH? WHA'S HPPNN?

NO, *DON'T!* SHE'S *SICK.*
YEAH, FROM THAT SHIT YOU BEEN SMOKING.

WHRER GOINN'?
SHHH... YOU'RE ALL RIGHT. I GOT'CHA.

HRR...

HURRRK!

PISS OFF! YOU NEVER SEEN A SICK GIRL BEFORE?

HERE WE GO, GIRLIE. SEE, MISSION DELORES?
ALMOST HOME SAFE WITH YOUR MAMA.
MY... MAMA? NO...
IT'S OKAY. SHE'S GONNA TAKE CARE OF YOU.

LOOK WHO I FOUND.
CARMEN!
HUHHNN?

SHE IS... DRUNK?
HRRNO.
SHE'S SICK, I THINK.

GRACIAS, GRACIAS.
SHE LIE DOWN, FEEL BETTER.
YOU KNOW, MAYBE A DOCTOR WOULD--
HERE, HERE. BONUS FOR YOU. THANK YOU!

BYE, BYE.
CLICK

YOU LOOK...
AND SMELL
LIKE SHIT.

MAYBE.
BUT I FOUND
THE GIRL.

NOW, THAT'S
WHY I LOVE YOU,
BABY.
WHY'S
THAT?
I CAN'T
EVER PIN YOU
DOWN.

MWAH!

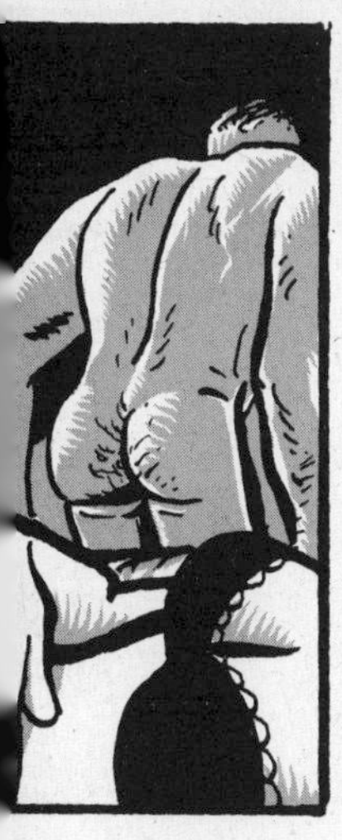

HEY, SO HERE'S TO ENDING THIS HORSESHIT WAR WITH THE GOOKS, HUH?

HORSESHIT WAR?

HEY, HEY, NO OFFENSE, BUT THIS "RED MENACE" CRAPOLA IS FOR THE BIRDS.

I MEAN, BACK IN THE DAY WE **KNEW** WHO OUR ENEMY WAS. AM I RIGHT?

THIS WHAT YOU WANT?
FUCK YOU, PALOOKA.

NO.
GUHKK.

FUCK YOU.
MRRMF!

RELAX.
I'LL WATCH THE NOSE.

THIS TIME.

HELLO, FRANK.

IT LOOKS LIKE YOU HAVE SOME GENTLEMAN CALLERS.

They tell me her name's Teresa Ramos. An actress who--

... DOES... *DID* THOSE COMMERCIALS ON MEXICAN RADIO.

Then they tell me she's the mother of three. All SONS.

They tell me they know I was there with "a drunk girl."

All they ask about is the girl.

WHO IS SHE?
HOW'D YOU KNOW HER?
WHERE IS SHE?

I just let 'em keep on askin'.

ALL I KNOW IS--
--SHE CALLED HERSELF MAGDA. SHE HIRED FRANK TO FIND HER DAUGHTER.

AND IF YOU THINK FRANK HAD ANYTHING TO DO WITH... THIS--
--YOU GOTTA BE MONGOLOID.

OH, REALLY? AND HOW'S THAT?
'CAUSE HE WAS WITH ME AFTER HE DROPPED CARMEN OFF.

REALLY? I DON'T REMEMBER HIM BEING THERE WHEN WE CAME BY AT THREE O'CLOCK IN THE A.M.

SO, WHERE WERE YOU, FRANKIE?

AND THIS GIRL, THIS CARMEN. WHERE'D FRANK FIND HER?
I DUNNO. I NEVER SAW HER.
SO HOW DO YOU KNOW THIS GIRL REALLY EXISTS?

LOOK, OFFICER, YOU DON'T UNDER-STAND, THIS IS ALL MY FAULT.
FRANK DIDN'T EVEN WANNA TAKE THE CASE. I INSISTED.

UH-HUH.
AND HOW LONG HAVE YOU BEEN WORKING FOR FRANK GRISSEL, MISS VALENTINE?
SEVEN YEARS.
UH-HUH. AND HOW LONG HAVE YOU BEEN... COHABITATING?

SEVEN YEARS.
AFTER YOU HIRED HIM TO GET PROOF OF YOUR THEN-HUSBAND'S INFIDELITIES, WHICH GOT YOU A HANDSOME ALIMONY.

THAT WHY YOU'VE NEVER MARRIED GRISSEL? DON'T WANT THE GRAVY TRAIN TO STOP?
THIS IS GETTING FISHY. HOW D'YOU KNOW ALL THIS?

THIS ISN'T ABOUT WHAT I KNOW, MISS VALENTINE.
DID YOU KNOW, UP UNTIL SHE DIED IN A GREEN BAY NUTHOUSE LAST YEAR, YOUR FRANKIE-BABY WAS STILL MARRIED TO THE WIFE HE LEFT THIRTY YEARS AGO?

THAT'S WHAT I THOUGHT.
SO IT SEEMS TO ME THAT...

"... YOU DON'T REALLY KNOW FRANK GRISSEL AFTER ALL."

THIS IS GOING NOWHERE.
WELL, PUT THE SCREWS IN, DETECTIVE.

OKAY, LET'S TRY THIS AGAIN, GRISSEL.
WHERE'D YOU FIND THE GIRL?

SMACK

C'MON. WHERE'D YOU FIND HER, FRANK?

SMACK

OH, YOU LIKE THAT, HUH? THEN YOU'RE GONNA LOVE THIS.
UH, DETECTIVE?

YEAH, WHAT IS IT, CLARENCE?
GRISSEL'S LAWYER'S HERE AND HE WANTS--
LAWYER? HOW? HE WASN'T GIVEN A--

EXCUSE ME. AM I TO UNDERSTAND YOU WITHHELD COUNSEL FOR MY CLIENT, DETECTIVE?
I...

WELL, UNLESS YOU WANT TO DISCUSS THAT CONSTITUTIONAL INDISCRETION, THE FRESH WELTS ON MY CLIENT'S FACE, OR THE FACT THAT HE HAS YET TO BE FORMALLY CHARGED--

--I THINK OUR TIME HERE IS DONE.

OKAY, SO WHAT'S THE CATCH? ALL THAT FANCY SHYSTER-ING CAN'T BE PRO BONO.
THE TERM "SHYSTER" IS DEGRADING NOT ONLY TO MY PROFESSION, BUT MY CREED, MR. GRISSEL.
YOU BET IT IS, BUDDY. NOW, WHAT'S THE CATCH?

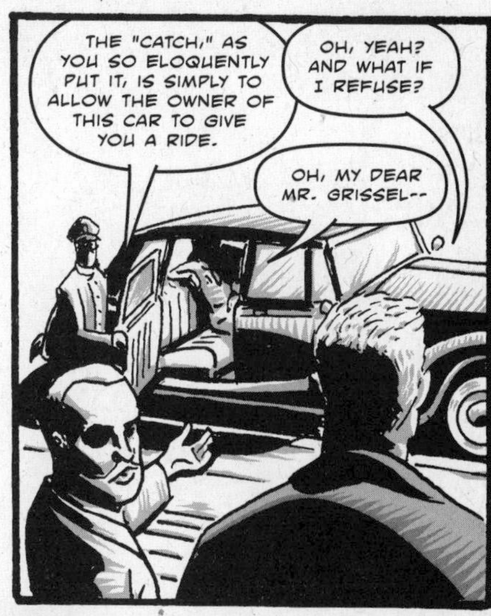

THE "CATCH," AS YOU SO ELOQUENTLY PUT IT, IS SIMPLY TO ALLOW THE OWNER OF THIS CAR TO GIVE YOU A RIDE.
OH, YEAH? AND WHAT IF I REFUSE?
OH, MY DEAR MR. GRISSEL--

-- THERE ARE SOME OFFERS THAT A MAN ***CAN'T*** REFUSE.

NOW WOULD YOU PLEASE DO ME THE PLEASURE OF COMING INSIDE?

THAT S.O.B.

BONE.
YES, COLONEL?

GET DADDY'S CADDY.

The first time I been in a Rolls. Never thought it'd be with...
I KNOW ALL ABOUT YOU.

... a Chinese broad with an English accent.
OH, I'M RIVETED, MR. GRISSEL, DO TELL.
YOU'RE A SHIPPING HEIRESS OUT'A HONG KONG.
AND WITH BUSINESS BOOMING HERE SINCE THEY STARTED LETTING CHINAMEN BACK IN THE COUNTRY, YOU BEEN ABLE TO COVER FOR WHAT YOU'RE REALLY BRINGIN' IN.

AND WHAT'S THAT?
OH, I GOT IDEAS. BUT YOUR BOOKKEEPER'S WHORE STOLE HERSELF SOME PROOF.
SO YOU HIRED THE ACTRESS TO HIRE ME TO FIND THE WHORE.
THEN THE BOOKKEEPER AND THE ACTRESS WIND UP DEAD, THE WHORE GOES MISSING, AND NOW YOU'RE TAKING ME FOR A RIDE... AGAIN.

HOW AM I DOIN' SO FAR...
...LADY TZE?

HA-HA-HA-HA!
OH, MY! THE WAY YOU PRONOUNCED MY NAME, IT'S LIKE...

LIKE WHAT?
LIKE I'M THE "LADY TEASE."

WHO SAYS YOU AIN'T?

I'M IN TROUBLE, MR. GRISSEL.

OH, YEAH? I KNOW A DOCTOR.
THAT'S HARDLY THE KIND OF TROUBLE I MEANT.
I GOT MORE'N ENOUGH OF YOUR KIND'A TROUBLE, THANK YOU VERY MUCH.

THE WAY YOU DEALT WITH THE POLICE WAS... IMPRESSIVE.

HERE--

-- YOU'VE BLOOD ON YOUR LIP.
MAY I?

ENOUGH. WHERE'S THIS OFFER I CAN'T REFUSE?

I... I NEED YOU, FRANK.
THERE'S NO ONE ELSE I CAN TRUST.

AH, CHRIST, LADY, THAT OLD ROUTINE?
TRUST ME? YOU DON'T EVEN KNOW ME.

I KNOW YOU'RE SMART ENOUGH TO KEEP YOUR MOUTH SHUT, YOUR EYES OPEN, AND YOUR ARMS STRONG.
A WOMAN IN MY POSITION CAN USE A MAN LIKE YOU.
OH, YEAH? AND WHAT KINDA MAN DO YOU LIKE TO USE?

A MAN WITH NEEDS.
A beautiful woman waves what must be five G's under my nose and the first thing I think is--

-- there's somebody out there willing to pay MORE.

NEED A RIDE, MISS?

PISS OFF, JACKASS.
I AIN'T WORK--

OH! OH, MY GOODNESS.
MY LANGUAGE. I'M SORRY. I HAD NO IDEA IT WAS...

...YOU.
ALL GOD'S CHILDREN MAKE MISTAKES, MY DEAR. SIMPLY A SAMARITAN OFFERING A LADY A LIFT.

NOTHING *NEFARIOUS.* I PROMISE.

I'M NOT GOING FAR, BUT THANK YOU.
THIS IS A REAL TREAT.
PLEASURE'S ALL MINE.

I NEED YOU TO RETURN WHAT THE GIRL STOLE.
THAT *HUSH* MONEY?

AND WHAT IS THAT, EXACTLY?
LEDGERS. RECORDS OF *BUSINESS* TRANSACTIONS.
UH-HUH, AND THIS *BUSINESS...* IT WITH ANY PARTY IN PARTICULAR?

DRIVER! PULL OVER.

WAIT, FRANK, WHAT'RE YOU DOING?
IF YOU AIN'T GONNA BE STRAIGHT WITH ME, TZE, THEN OUR BUSINESS IS DONE.
NO, **PLEASE.** THERE'S A LOT MORE WHERE THAT CAME FROM.

SOME THINGS AIN'T ABOUT MONEY. EVEN TO "MEN LIKE ME."

WELL, IF YOU CHANGE YOUR MIND, YOU KNOW WHERE TO FIND ME.
GOOD DAY, MR. GRISSEL.

WHO IS SHE?
AH CHRIST, DON'T START, 'RETTA.

THAT WOMAN WHO PICKED YOU UP. SHE'S THE REASON YOU GO OUT AT NIGHT, ISN'T SHE?
DON'T BE CRAZY.

CRAZY?
CRAZY LIKE YOUR WIFE WENT AFTER YOU LEFT HER?!
WHO TOLD YOU THAT?

HOW MANY OTHER SECRETS YOU GOT IN THAT CLOSET, FRANK?!

GODDAMMIT! ARE YOU FUCKING HER?!

IT'S BECAUSE SHE'S *RICH*, ISN'T IT?
ISN'T IT?!

YOU'RE GONNA USE HER UP LIKE YOU USED *ME!*
STOP.
LET GO OF ME!

SHHH.
OH, GOD, FRANK... I...
SOB!

TOO TIGHT. I CAN'T--
HERE, I'LL--
FORGET IT.
FLIK!

OH, GOD, FRANK. NO.
SHRRRRRRIIIP!
OH, GOD, FRANK. YES!

HNH.
AH-HH.
HNH.
AH-HH!
KISS ME, FRANK. JUST THIS ONCE.
I DON'T LIKE KISSING.
HURRN!

FEEL BETTER NOW?
SURE.

GOOD.
YOU KNOW WHO GAVE ME A RIDE TODAY, FRANK?
WHO?

COLONEL THORPE, HIMSELF.

I GOTTA GO.
YOU OWE ME FOR A NEW SKIRT.

Some things fall down.
And others keep standing.
Thorpe Mansion. The house that piety built.
The Great Quake couldn't tear her down.
But I got a hunch what's in Tze's ledgers could.
RIINNNG!

HELLO! AFTERNOON!
UH, YEAH, I--
YOU WANT MISTER COLONEL, YES?
YES, I--

Funny, I figured Thorpe woulda got a real tea-and-biscuits kinda butler.
Not some two-bit immigrant who'll let ANYONE in.
YES, YES, PLEASE. COME IN, THIS WAY.

And them maids. Jesus, they's just fresh off the boat, or what?

MR. BONE! HERE--
OH, UH...
-- HE HERE FOR MISTER COLONEL.

I'LL TAKE CARE OF IT, CHAN.
OKAY, OKAY. GOODBYE.

YOU SHOULD GO.

NOW.

WHHOOSHH

OH MY GOODNESS.
WHAT DO WE HAVE HERE? I DO LOVE SURPRISES.

MR. GRISSEL, ISN'T IT?
UH... YEAH. THAT'S RIGHT, MR. THORPE.
OH, SHOOT... CALL ME COLONEL. EVERYONE DOES.

IT'S A PLEASURE, MR. GRISSEL.

NOW, PLEASE JOIN ME IN MY DEN. I TAKE IT YOU HAVE BUSINESS TO DISCUSS.

IT'S NOT MUCH, I KNOW.
BUT IT'S COZY.
YEAH... COZY.

THEM PICTURES. JAMES THORPE ONE, TWO, AND THREE.
AIN'T THERE A LITTLE JIMMY THORPE NUMBER FOUR?
THE LORD HAS BIGGER PLANS FOR MY LEGACY THAN BASE REPRODUCTION.

YOU'D THINK HE'D HAVE **BETTER** THINGS TO DO.

HANDS ON THE DESK.
WHAP
HEY!

MY APOLOGIES, BUT A MAN IN MY POSITION CAN'T BE TOO CAREFUL WITH STRANGERS.
LEMME SAVE YOU TIME--

THERE'S HEAT UNDER MY LEFT BREAST.

YOU FOUND IT.

ANYTHING ELSE?

GO FISH.

OH.

WHAT? SOMETHING INTEREST YOU, BONE?

NO, COLONEL. HE'S CLEAN.

CLEAN? JE PEUX SENTIR SES ORDURES D'ICI.

PARDONER ODEUR MI. MIN COME VOS LI SAVEZ. J'AI PASSE LI NUTE EN PR'JHON.
OH, YOU SPEAK FRENCH. OR SOME... VERSION THEREOF. WHAT IS THAT? QUEBECOIS?

MY POP WAS A BELGIAN WALLOON.
WALLOON?
GRACIOUS, I DIDN'T KNOW THERE WAS SUCH A THING. YOU GROW MORE FASCINATING BY THE MINUTE, MR. GRISSEL.

NOW PLEASE HAVE A SIT-DOWN. I HUNGER FOR ALL THE FASCINATING THINGS YOU HAVE TO SAY.
WELL--
AND IN ENGLISH, PLEASE. AS MUCH AS I'D LIKE TO, I JUST COULDN'T FOLLOW YOUR BASTARD TONGUE.

WELL, MY ENGLISH AIN'T SO GOOD NEITHER, SO I'LL JUST CUT THE SHIT AND GET TO THE MEAT.

I DUNNO AND DON'T CARE WHO KILLED THE ACTRESS, BUT DOLLARS TO DONUTS, YOU GOT THE GIRL.
BUT YOU BET CARMEN'S TOO SICK T'SAY HER OWN NAME, LET ALONE WHERE SHE STASHED THE DRAGON LADY'S LEDGERS.
FUNNY HOW A JUNKIE WHORE WHO DON'T EVEN KNOW ENGLISH HARDLY, KNEW JUST WHICH CHINESE BOOKS TO NICK... TRES MYSTERIEUX, NON?

I'M SURE I DON'T KNOW WHAT YOU MEAN, BUT IF I DID, I SUPPOSE YOU'D OFFER YOUR SERVICES TO FIND SAID "LEDGERS."
YOU'D SUPPOSE RIGHT.

I TAKE IT, REGARDLESS OF YOUR APPEARANCE, YOUR SERVICES AREN'T CHEAP?
TEN. LARGE.
THAT'S SUBSTANTIAL.

YOU CAN HANDLE IT.
AND MORE.

MORE? YOU GREEDY PIG, YOU!
LET THE GIRL GO.

HA HA HA!
YOU'RE OVER-REACHING, MR. GRISSEL.

AND LIKE THE ARCHANGEL LUCIFER--

--YOU WILL BE STRUCK DOWN.

ALL I CAN OFFER YOU NOW IS THE GIFT OF LIFE. SO, WHERE ARE THE LEDGERS?

FUCK YOU.

REMARKABLE SPECIMEN, ISN'T HE?
I CALL HIM MY "BEAUTIFUL BONE."
ALL THOSE YEARS IN THE RING...
... AND GOD KEPT HIS FACE FLAWLESS. UNTOUCHED.
WHOOOOM
YOUR FACE, MR. GRISSEL, SHOWS YOUR EVERY FAILURE.

RARRGH!
WHUD!!
KRAK

I PULLED SOME STRINGS TO GET BONE AN HONORABLE DISCHARGE.
CRAZY'S BETTER THAN WHAT THEY REALLY CHARGED HIM WITH.
SODOMY.
BUT WITH MY GUIDANCE AND CHRIST'S FORGIVENESS...
... HE'S AS THE LORD INTENDED.
A REAL MAN.
AND UNLESS YOU WANT HIM TO POUND YOU STRAIGHT TO HELL, YOU'LL TELL ME--

TELL YOU? HUH?
I look at Bone.
He shows me what he wants me to do.
Seems unbelievable.
He WANTS me to DO IT.
I won't say no.

I almost gag on my heart.
FLK!
SLSSH!
Finally, the Big Boy lets ME FUCK HIM.
NO!

AGH!
WHOOHM!

CHAN! STOP HIM! DON'T LET HIM--

SMACK!

SOMEBODY STOP HIM!!!

YEAH. WELCOME TO SAN FRANCISCO, FOLKS.
ENJOY THE VIEW.

Every time I think things'll turn around for me... they end up straight in the shitter.
Now I REALLY gotta find them ledgers.

Carmen's Bohemian buddy's long gone after my last visit.

Johns Grill
JAZZ
I hate to do it, but I don't know where else to go.
Grill
FOOD

BLACK
CAFE
Back to the Godblessed BLACK CAT.

It catches my eye like a spook.

For a second I think it's her. The little blondie split open in the morgue.
I WANT it to be her, but it ain't her. And that ain't no John, neither.

It's the HEAD-SHRINKER.
COME WITH ME, PLEASE.
NO, DON'T. I CAN'T. PLEASE!

I JUST WANT TO TALK. C'MON, THIS ISN'T YOU.
I DON'T WANNA BE ME.

I HAVE TO, OR ELSE I'LL...

OR ELSE, WHAT? DID HE THREATEN YOU?
DID HE TOUCH YOU?

HE'S A SICK MAN, YOU UNDERSTAND? EVEN THE CATHOLICS WON'T--
SPEAK OF THE DEVIL.
--OH, SHIT.

YOU! I TOLD YOU--
I WON'T LET YOU FILL THIS KID'S HEAD UP WITH ANY MORE OF YOUR MEDIEVAL BULLSHIT, FISCHER.

I AM MORE CONCERNED WITH SAVING SOULS THAN CORRUPTING MINDS FOR PERSONAL GAIN, DOCTOR.
PERSONAL GAIN? HOW D'YOU--
I AM DOING GOD'S WORK. WHOSE WORK ARE YOU DOING?

COME. WE'VE INDULGED THIS FALSE PROPHET LONG ENOUGH.
UH!

MY HAIR!
LEAVE IT.

GOD-FUCKING-BLESSIT.

ROARING 20's
CONDOR
Lounge
BIG AL'S

ROARING 20's
CONDOR
Lounge

EXIT

YOU GONNA CREEP AROUND ALL NIGHT, FRANK GRISSEL, P.I.?
OR DO YOU WANT TO COME IN?

RELAX.
I'LL GO EASY
ON YOU.

TELL ME
ABOUT YOUR
CHILDHOOD.

YOU ARE A **DEEPLY DISTURBED** MAN. A **DANGER** TO SOCIETY.

AND YOU'RE FULL'A SHIT.

SO YOU BELIEVE PROWLING FOR UNDERAGE PROSTITUTES AND STALKING OTHER YOUNG WOMEN ARE JUST PEACHY-KEEN THINGS TO DO?

I WASN'T...

THE SONUVA BITCH.

HE'S GOT A ***STASH***... I KNOW IT.
C'MON, C'MON...

CAN'T BE ALL...
HUH?

WHAT THE--?
KRRRKK

OH, FRANK...
NO!

WHO SAYS I GOT A GIRLFRIEND?
WELL, SOMEBODY'S BUYING VAN HEUSEN SHIRTS FOR YOU TO BLEED ALL OVER.

I BET IT SURE BEATS WORKING THE DOCKS ON GREEN BAY IN JANUARY, RIGHT?
TRY AUGUST, FUCKING HUMIDITY'S LIKE BREATHING UNDERWATER.
NO WONDER YOU TOOK THE EASY WAY OUT.
EASY WAY?

OH, DON'T BE COY. IT DOESN'T SUIT YOU. YOU KNOW WHAT I MEAN--
-- SEDUCING WOMEN OF SOME MEANS, BLEEDING THEM DRY, AND THEN MOVING ON TO THE NEXT ONE.

YOU DON'T KNOW NOTHIN' ABOUT ME.

OH, COME NOW, FRANK, I **STUDY** WHORES FOR A LIVING.

WHAT'D YOU CALL ME?!

YOU ARE WHAT YOU ARE, FRANK.

FUCK THIS.
I COME HERE TO HELP A LITTLE GIRL, NOT BE INSULTED BY SOME MAN-HATING QUACK.

I AM NOT A QUACK!

WHO CARES WHAT'CHA ARE? A LYING BITCH'S A LYING BITCH.
ME? I'M A LIAR?

YOU ARE WHAT'CHA ARE, DOC. AND IF YOU DON'T KNOW IT--
-- YOU'RE A PRETTY SHITTY HEADSHRINKER.

Physique PICTORIAL
Vim
TOMORROWS MAN
GOD HELP ME...
... THE SON OF A BITCH IS A FAG.
HRRM...
Vim
ARRRRRRRGH!

I...

...YOU'RE RIGHT.
PLEASE, MR. GRISSEL... STAY.

I APOLOGIZE, I'M VERY PROTECTIVE OF THE PEOPLE I'VE BEEN WORKING WITH.
SO, I WAS RIGHT. YOU DO KNOW CARMEN.
I ONLY MET HER ONCE. SHE WAS HIGH AS A KITE, I GAVE HER MY CARD. NEVER HEARD FROM HER. THAT'S ALL I KNOW.

AND LEMME GUESS, YOU MET HER...
... AT THE SAME GODDAMN PLACE YOU MET HER LI'L PANSY PAL, GREG.
AND THAT LITTLE BLONDIE THAT WAS GUTTED RIGHT ON THEIR DOORSTEP.
IS THAT WHY THAT FRUITY PRIEST'S SO MAD? YOU FLEECING HIS FLOCK?

THAT PRIEST IS NOTHING BUT A GLORIFIED PIMP AND HIS **SO-CALLED MINISTRY** IS A **WHITEWASHED TAX SHELTER** MASQUERA--

TELL IT TO **HERB CAEN.** RIGHT NOW THAT LITTLE GIRL NEEDS ME.

ALL RIGHT. SO, HOW CAN I... **HELP?**

OKAY, SO YOU KNOW WHORES, YEAH? HOW THEY THINK AND STUFF?
IT DEPENDS.
OKAY, SO SAY YOU WERE CARMEN AND YOU GOT YOUR MITTS ON SOMETHING REAL VALUABLE AND REAL DANGEROUS...

...WHERE'D YOU HIDE IT?
WELL, I'D...

...AH. OF COURSE. YOU ALMOST GOT ME.
AGAIN.

WHAT'RE YOU--
YOU'RE RIGHT. Y'KNOW, I DO KNOW HOW PROSTITUTES THINK.

THIS ISN'T ABOUT HER. THIS IS ABOUT YOU CASHING IN ON WHATEVER SHE STOLE FOR YOURSELF.

JEEZ, YOU REALLY ARE TRULY HOLLOW AND PATHETIC AND--
THAT AIN'T SO. SHE'S SICK AND--
OH, CUT THE SHIT, FRANK.
WHY RISK YOUR LIFE FOR A MEXICAN STREETWALKER WHEN YOU WALKED AWAY FROM YOUR OWN DAUGHTER?

WAIT, HOW'D YOU KNOW ABOUT--

CLICK

TAKE A GUESS,
SHERLOCK.

FUCK YOU.
WELL, WELL, MISS VALENTINE.
HUH?
QUITE A MESS YOU'VE MADE.

NEED A HAND, MY DEAR?
I... NO. NO THANK YOU, I...

YOU GOTTA BE SHITTIN' ME...

BETTY?

HELLO, DADDY.

BETTY... I... I'M...
SAVE IT.

BEFORE I END YOUR MISERABLE, GOOD-FOR-NOTHING LIFE, I JUST WANT YOU TO ASK YOURSELF--
--WAS SHE WORTH IT?
WHAT? WHO?

THE BITCH YOU LEFT US FOR. WHO WAS SHE, FRANK?
I... UH...

WHO WAS SHE?!

STEVE HOGANSON.

MY GOD.

YOU'RE A FAIRY.

WHAP

UNGH!
NO!
BANG
CRASH!

I run. Out of instinct.

VIO
And it hits me.

I ain't got NOWHERE to go.
NO ONE who'll have me.
I never done NOTHING right. My whole life.

I'm just a piece of shit in this city full of shit.
I wanna tear my skin off. Turn into somebody different.

I gotta get outta this town.
And then, for the second time today, I see...

TZE SHIPPING

... a way out.

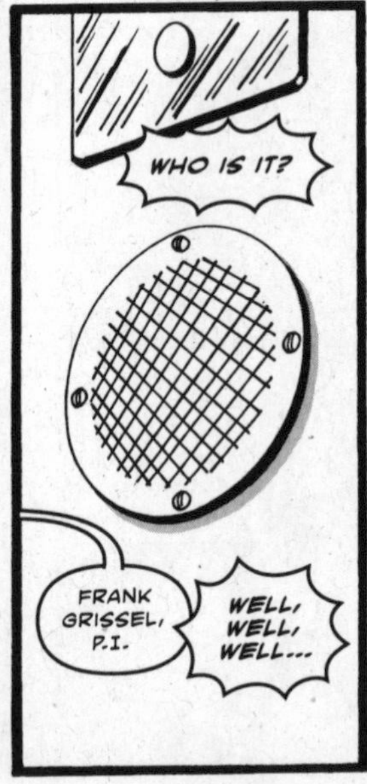

WHO IS IT?
FRANK GRISSEL, P.I.
WELL, WELL, WELL...

... DO COME IN, MR. GRISSEL.
I'VE BEEN EXPECTING YOU.

BONSOIR, ETRANGER.

LOOKS LIKE YOU COULD USE A HIGHBALL...

"... AND MAYBE A DRINK, TOO."
"BEHOLD!" MISS VALENTINE, "THOU ART FAIR."
WELL, JEEZ, COLONEL, BETWEEN BUYING ME THIS DRESS, CALLING ME "MISS," AND INSERTING ME INTO THE SONG OF SOLOMON--
-- YOUR FLATTERY WILL GET YOU EVERY-WHERE.

AND YOU KNOW YOUR SCRIPTURE, TOO?
IMPRESSIVE.
I WAS A GOOD CATHOLIC GIRL... ONCE.
HAH-HA! AND WHY'D YOU FALL FROM THE FAITH?
YOU WANT THE TRUTH?
I EXPECT NOTHING LESS FROM YOU, MY DEAR.

GOD IS TOO CRUEL TO BELIEVE IN.

OH, YOU'RE WRONG. GOD ISN'T CRUEL--
--MAN IS.

SO, WHO WAS HE? YOUR FATHER? A DRUNKEN UNCLE, PERHAPS?
NO. YOUR HUSBAND, I THINK. THE ADULTERER.

EX-HUSBAND.
AND IT WASN'T HIS CHEATING THAT...

... WAITAMINUTE.
I DIDN'T TELL YOU ABOUT--
MSSSHH...

MOHH WHUNN?
GASP!
WHAT'S--?

MOHH WHUNN?
MORE WINE! YES, THANKS.
AW, JEEZ, HONEY, WHO SLUGGED YOU?

ROOT CANAL.
THEY COME OVER WITH SUCH BAD TEETH, YOU KNOW. I DO WHAT I CAN.

THE GOOD LORD HAS BLESSED ME WITH SO MUCH. AND THERE ARE SO MANY PEOPLE IN NEED... ESPECIALLY IN THIS CITY.
HAD SODOM A MAN LIKE ME GUIDING IT, IT WOULD STILL BE STANDING.
AH, C'MON. SAN FRANCISCO AIN'T ALL THAT BAD.
WELL, I'M SURE MR. GRISSEL IS EXPLICIT IN THE DETAILS OF HIS LESS... SAVORY CASES.
REALLY? SO, HE HASN'T TOLD YOU--
HAH! FRANK DOESN'T TELL ME SQUAT ABOUT SQUAT.

COLONEL, THE INFECTION IS... OH... UH...
YES, FATHER FISCHER?
... MAY I HAVE A WORD?

IS THERE ANYTHING ELSE YOU NEED?
YEAH. 'CAUSA YOUR LITTLE GOOSECHASE... I GOTTA SKIP TOWN, TOOT SUITE.

AND YOU'RE COMING WITH ME.
WHAT? WHY WOULD I--
THE COLONEL'S GOT CARMEN. ONCE HE GETS HIS HANDS ON THEM LEDGERS, HE'LL DESTROY YOU AND TAKE IT ALL FOR HIMSELF.

SO, WHAT DO WE DO?
WE GO SOMEPLACE FAR AWAY FROM HERE AND NEVER COME BACK.

AND YOU'LL PROTECT ME?
YOU BET.

I HAVE A SHIP LEAVING FOR EUROPE TOMORROW NIGHT.

I DON'T KISS.
THAT'S ALL RIGHT...

...I DO.

MISS VALENTINE, YOU MUST EXCUSE ME.
IF YOU NEED, I COULD JUST GO--
NO, PLEASE. STAY.
AT LEAST ONE OF US WILL ENJOY A HOT MEAL.

IT'S YOU.

HUHHNN--

OW!

OHHH...
FUUUCK...

WHUMP

YOU'RE **BURNING UP,** CATHERINE. AND...
OH, GOD... THE BLOOD'S...
... AND THAT **SMELL...**
HRRN...

OKAY, OKAY...
YOU'RE GONNA BE OKAY.
LET'S GET YOU--

HOW THE HELL DO YOU GET OUT OF THESE?

MISS VALENTINE.

WHEN YOU TURN YOUR BACK TO GOD...
HE TURNS HIS BACK ON *YOU*.

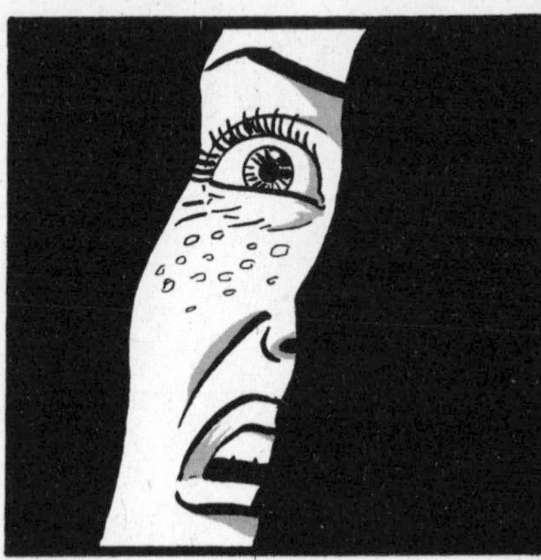

HRRN? M'GUN? HOW'D--

OH. SHIT.
That cunt-eyed bitch set me up.
She was working with the phony Colonel all along.

Can't help it. it's just what I do.

WHAM!

I SURVIVE.

After all's said 'n done--

-- I'm just a SELFISH BASTARD.

One'a these days I'll pay the piper for it.

ARRGH!
BANG!

Just not today.

'Cause lucky for me...

... today's the day...

... we pulled a draw with the Gooks.

A DRAW.
And you'd think it's fuckin' VJ-DAY.
Everybody wants to be treated SPECIAL.

I ain't different. Tze sure as shit played that angle.
Led by the nose since that actress came in my door.
Looking for a lost "daughter."

They done their homework.
Means they know about Betty. But dollars to donuts they don't know the kid is...

... DR. GREY.
YET.
YOU'RE BLEEDING.
NO SHIT.
YOU'VE BEEN SHOT!
YEAH, SORRY, DOC. COPS BEAT Y'TO IT.
THIS IS BAD.
YOU NEED A DOCTOR.

WELL, I AIN'T CALLIN' YA DOC FOR NOTHIN'.
I'M NOT... THAT KIND OF--

C'MON, EVEN I KNOW HEAD-SHRINKERS CAN STITCH--
I CAN'T HELP YOU.

LOOK, YOU WAS BETTER OFF WITH NO FATHER THAN WITH ONE THAT'S...
... UH, YOU KNOW...
... AND SEE? LOOK AT'CHA. A DOCTOR.
MY BETTY'S A--

I'M NOT!
I'M NOT A DOCTOR!
YOU DIG ME NOW, DADDY-O?

YOU...
YOU AIN'T--?
NO! JESUS, THE IRONY!

AFTER EVERYTHING I DID NOT TO, I STILL END UP JUST LIKE YOU.
A BIG FAT FRAUD.

AT LEAST YOU AIN'T A DRUNK.

HURN...
THIS IS NOT LOOKING GOOD...
JESUS.
ISN'T THERE ANYONE?

... YOU **HAVEN'T** PISSED OFF, FRANK?
THEY'RE NOT ONLY FRAMING YOU FOR 'RETTA AND THE CHIQUITA, BUT FOR THE ACTRESS AND THE GUTTED BLONDIE, TOO.
THE BLONDIE? WHAT'S SHE GOT TO--
YOUR PRINTS WERE ON HER LIGHTER, AND THE KNIFE USED ON THEM BOTH WAS ALSO USED ON...

... CHIQUITA HERE.
AND THE "BLONDIE"-- HER NAME WAS **MAUREEN,** BY THE WAY-- SHE WAS EVISCERATED LIKE THIS, TOO?

YES'M. 'CEPT BLONDIE DIDN'T HAVE ANY LADY PARTS 'CAUSE THE SICK-O **TOOK 'EM.**
CHIQUITA HERE NEVER **HAD NONE** TO **BEGIN WITH.**
OH.
OH... SO... THAT'S... **MANMADE,** HUH?

MANMADE? YOU SAYIN' CARMEN'S A... LIKE, WHAT'S-HER... THAT, Y'KNOW, THAT HE-SHE SWEDE?
CHRISTINE JORGENSON. AND SHE'S DANISH.
YUP. THE SCANDIES SURE DO A TOP-NOTCH CHOP JOB. SOMEONE PAID A PRETTY PENNY FOR THIS ONE.

HER NASTY INFECTION WAS ON ACCOUNT'A SHE WAS USING HER NEW PUSS AS A HIDEY-HOLE.
I MUST'A NEGLECTED THIS KEY DETAIL IN MY REPORT.

DON'T MAKE ME REGRET IT, GRISSEL.

REGRET.

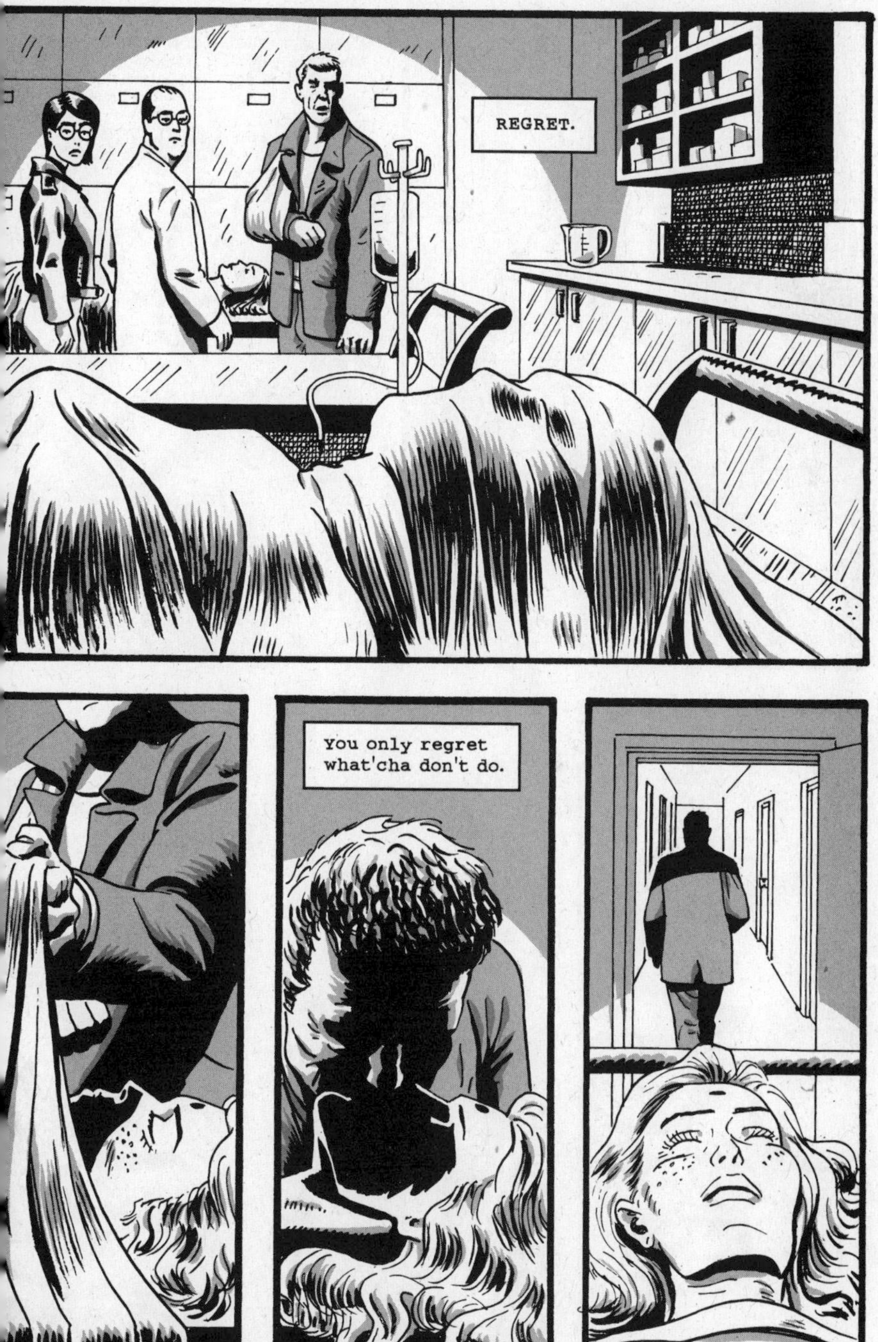

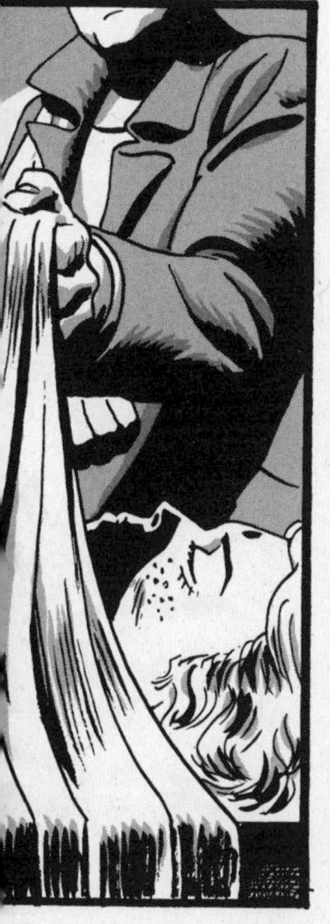

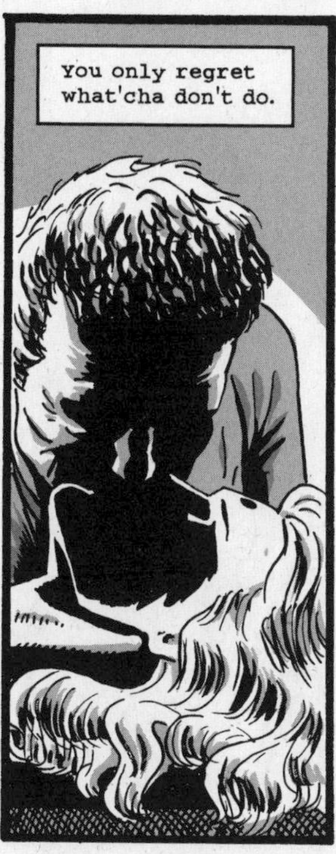
You only regret what'cha don't do.

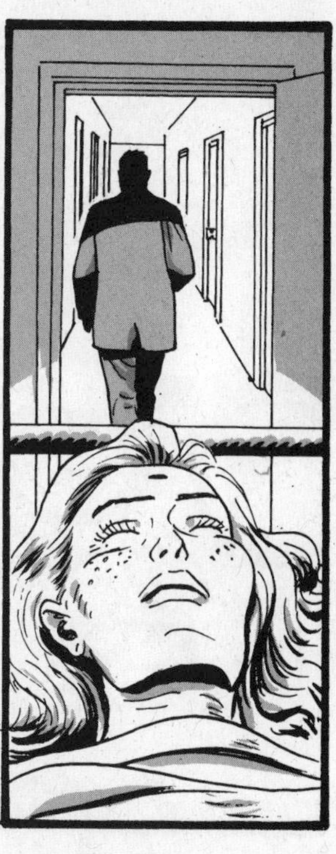

HOLD UP!
I'M COMING
WITH YOU.
NO WAY.
GO BE A FAKE
SHRINK IN SOME
OTHER 'BURG.
THIS IS WAY TOO
DANGEROUS.

LOOK, MOTHERFUCKER, THE "FATHER KNOWS BEST" BULLSHIT ENDED THE MINUTE YOU LEFT US FOR SOME COCKSUCKER NAMED STEVE.

SO DON'T CONCERN YOURSELF WITH MY WELL-BEING, NOW.

YOU STILL PACKIN' THAT HEAT?

HOTEL
STRATFORD
環亞酒店

YOU LIKE *BLEEDING*, PUNK?

I... I...
THE NUMBER. NOW.
FIF-FIFTEEN.

And BINGO.
16
15
The key fits.

Funny. I half-expect 'em to be solid gold, for all they're worth.
But, like everything else. 'Retta and all them lives boil down to...

... Just paper and ink.

CALL THE COPS AND YOU TELL 'EM-- "GRISSEL'S GOT THE COLONEL'S LEDGERS." YOU GOT THAT?
MESS IT UP, AND YOU BETTER DECIDE WHERE I FUCK YOU FIRST.
YES, SIR.

HOTEL
STRATFORD
YOU DONE SWELL, KITTEN.
AW, GEE. THANKS, "POP."

WAIT, WHAT'S THIS ONE MEAN?
CAN'T TELL. WHATEVER IT IS, IT WAS SENT TO COPENHAGEN.

SO, IF THE COLONEL'S USING THE TEASE'S BOATLOADS OF CHINKY TRINKETS AS A COVER FOR SMUGGLED DOPE AND ILLEGAL CHINAMEN... WHAT'S THEY PACKIN' OUT TO DENMARK?

OH, SHIT. ***CARMEN.***
BUT THERE'S DOZENS OF...
OH, SHIT. YOU'RE RIGHT. THE LAST ENTRY CAME RIGHT BACK HERE JUST TWO WEEKS AGO.

SO, NOT ONLY'S THE COLONEL CORNERED THE DOPE TRADE AND DODGING THE CHINESE EXCLUSION ACT, BUT HE'S ALSO TRAFFICKIN' IN ***HE-SHE'S?***
CHINESE ENGLISH
WHAT KINDA WEIRDOS ARE PAYIN' FOR THIS SICK SHIT?

APPARENTLY, REALLY, ***REALLY RICH*** ONES.

I stash the books.

And mail myself the key.
I keep Betty's little discovery for insurance.
And pick up some new heat on the way.

Then, as everybody else celebrates the end of a horseshit war--

-- sorry, make that a horseshit "CONFLICT"--

-- Me and Betty head to the piers.

If the Colonel'd got my message about the ledgers, I'd be deaf from the sound of flatfeet by now.

But there ain't no one. Not even a DECKHAND in sight.

Which says to me the sick ol' fuck don't want nobody to know about this.

UH-OH.
Okay, so, maybe not NOBODY.

YOU JUST DON'T LEARN.
I SHOULD KNOW...
...PRETTY BOYS MAKE GRAVES.

STOP.
OH, C'MON, IT'S SO OBVIOUS--

NO.
STAY HERE.
AND DO *WHAT?*
WHAT YOU SHOULD'A DONE TO ME...

... SHOOT FIRST AND ASK YOUR QUESTIONS LATER.
PEACHY ADVICE, *POP.*

JUST GODDAMN PEACHY.

UHK-GUUH--

MAY GOD **FORGIVE YOU** FOR FORSAKING HIM.

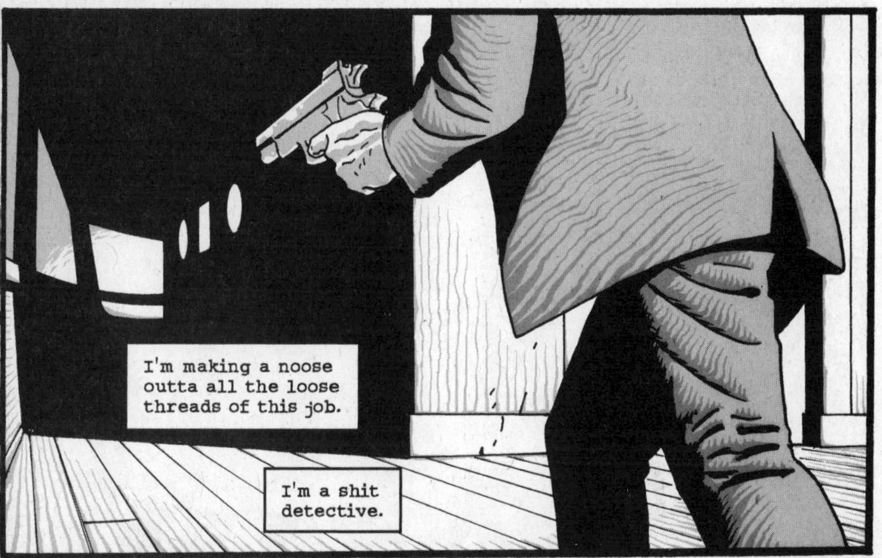
I'm making a noose outta all the loose threads of this job.
I'm a shit detective.

They could'a got some Pinkerton dick to find Carmen.
They didn't want a dick. They wanted a PATSY.

I might be a lotta shameful things.
But this dick ain't NOBODY'S patsy.

One look and them threads tighten up real quick around my neck.

Greg all doped-up in the same chair as Carmen.

The sick pig snapping pictures.

I'm blind and stupid. 'Course after all what happened, it all boils down to the blondie whore. MAUREEN...
She was MARKED.
They was watching. Saw me give her my Zippo and Saw their scapegoat.

But, why split her open and snatch up her whole kit-n-kaboodle, if she weren't no... Jorgenson?
Told me she was gonna be RICH, soon.
Blackmail? Couldn't be about them ledgers.

And you bet from the slim pickin's in her purse, she wasn't no LONG-TERM PLANNER.
I always say, if a whore don't carry rubbers, she's either looking for trouble, or...
... has already FOUND IT.
PUTAIN!

That's what was hacked outta her.
The LEGACY he never WANTED.
The blade used on her I got off'a Greggie, but that li'l queer don't got the balls or muscle for THAT sort'a job.

But, I bet'cha, under his frock, that so-called PRIEST'S got plenty of both.
GURRK!
"I WILL TEAR OFF YOUR VEILS AND SAVE MY PEOPLE FROM YOUR HANDS, AND THEY WILL NO LONGER FALL PREY TO YOUR POWER. THEN YOU WILL KNOW THAT I AM THE--"
KRAKK!
URRGH!

OUR FATHER WILL DENY HEAVEN TO THOSE WHO--
FUCK YOU! FUCK HEAVEN! AND...
BLAM!!!
--- FUCK YOUR FATHER!

WHAT--?

YOU!
I GUESS YOU WAS TOO BUSY TO GET MY MESSAGE.
MESSAGE? WHAT'RE YOU--

I GOT TZE'S LEDGERS.
KRAK!

Dunno why I think'a it. But once I do, NOTHIN' ELSE matters.
Not Betty, Greggie, Colonel or cops. nothin' else but...

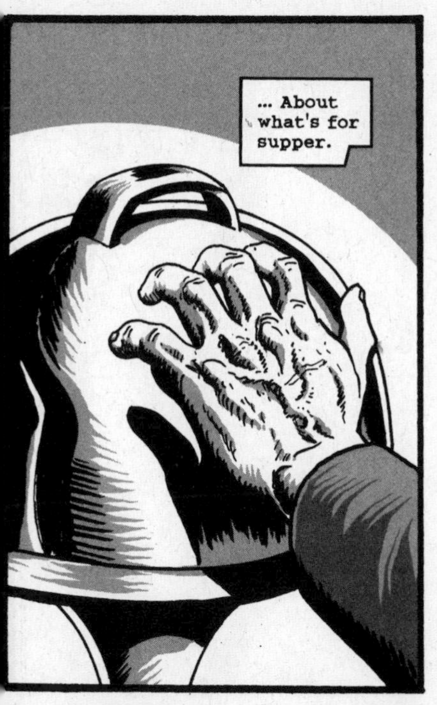

My gut empties in my throat.
I can almost hear the bent old fuck tellin' Greggie...

... "You are what you eat."

C'MON, KID--
NOOO DNNN'T... I'LL GO T'HELL...

DON'T BE *STUPID.*
UHN!
SMACK!

YOU'RE COMIN' WITH ME.
BUT...
BUT *WHAT?*

ONLY GIRLS'RE S'POSED TO LIKE GUYS.

DO I *LOOK* LIKE A *GIRL,* TO YOU?

WOW.
I'VE GOT SERIOUS DADDY ISSUES.

OH, MAN.
I LOST MY GLASSES.

HNNK!

DO YOU LIKE ME? THAT DAY IN THE ALLEY--
OH YEAH, SURE. YOU'RE ACES.
NOW C'MON, WE GOTTA...
FRANK GRISSEL.

DROP YOUR GUN AND GET YOUR HANDS UP.

YOU DON'T UNDERSTAND--
THE KID'S DONE NOTHING WRONG.

--HE'S DONE EVERYTHING WRONG.
HE NEEDS TO BE REBORN.

THERE AIN'T GREASE ENOUGH FOR THEM COP'S PALMS IF THEY'S TO KNOW WHAT YOU PLANNED TO DO TO LI'L GREGGIE-ANN, HERE.
GO AHEAD, NO ONE WILL BELIEVE YOU.

HA! COPS'RE WORSE GOSSIPS THAN PREACHER'S WIVES.
AND THEY GOT GOBS TO GAB IF THEY GOT A GANDER OF THIS...
FREEZE!

RELAX, COPPERS. IT'S JUST PAPER, SEE?
JUST A LITTLE CLIENT LIST TUCKED IN THEM LEDGERS...

GIVE ME THAT!
I DUNNO, SOME'A THESE NAMES ARE PRETTY RECOGNIZABLE, EVEN TO A DUMB-SHIT WALLOON LIKE ME.

BE A SHAME I SHOULD ACCIDENTALLY BLURT ONE OUT AND WHAT HE BOUGHT.

THE BOY CAN GO.

FORGET ABOUT ME. JUST SCRAM, KID.
WHAT ABOUT YOU?
AND ALL OF YOU OFFICERS CAN KINDLY WAIT ON THE DOCK.

THANK YOU SO MUCH, GENTLEMEN. WON'T BE A MOMENT.

NOW, THE LIST, IF YOU WILL.
AND THEN WE'LL DISCUSS YOUR TERMS.

A DEAL'S A DEAL.
WAIT!

EVERYTHING IN THOSE LEDGERS IS ***MINE.***

HAND IT OVER, FRANK. OR THE SHRINK GOES IN THE DRINK.

NOW, FRANK. THE LIST, IF YOU WILL?
YOUR DAUGHTER'S HEAVIER THAN SHE APPEARS.
DAUGHTER?
YESSIR.

AND YET, YOU DON'T RUSH TO SAVE HER?
I NEVER ASKED FOR A KID.
THEY JUST SUCK YOU DRY AND SHOVE IT IN YOUR FACE LATER, RIGHT?

WELL, WELL. YOU AND I ARE MORE ALIKE THAN PERHAPS EITHER OF US WOULD LIKE TO ADMIT, GRISSEL.
I COULD USE A MAN LIKE YOU.
FUNNY. WHERE'VE I HEARD THAT COME-ON BEFORE?

YOUR HEARTLESS FATHER ACT DOESN'T FOOL ME, FRANK.
NOW GIVE ME THE LIST OR I DROP HER IN THE BAY.

GO AHEAD. I LEFT HER FOR DEAD TWENTY-FIVE YEARS AGO.

YOU'LL REGRET THIS!

NO...

... IT AIN'T REGRET.

BLAM!

San Francisco Bay's cold.
So cold it sucks the life outta you.
It's partly what keeps the cons on Alcatraz.
But, still--
-- it ain't no GREEN BAY in January.

Remember back a piece, what I said about them "THREE F's" that men'll do anything for?
I was wrong.
I forgot one.
FAMILY.
GASP!

WHA--?
WHERE--?
SHHH...
IT'S OKAY.

YOU BEEN OUT FOR AWHILE.
WHAT HAPPENED...?
GOTTA TIE UP SOME LOOSE ENDS, THEN I'LL FILL YOU IN.

EVERYTHING'S PACKED AND I'M ON THE 12:15 TO L.A.
AND THE *PLAN?*
WESTERN UNION. EVERY TUESDAY AT FOUR.

NOW, G'WAY, BOY. YA BOTHER ME.

HERE'S WHAT I WANT.

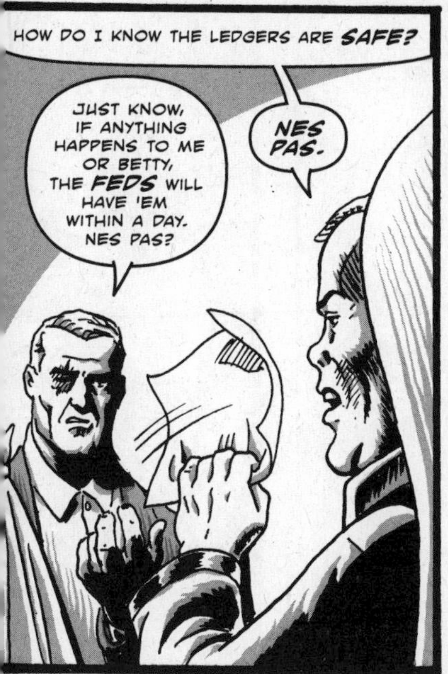

HOW DO I KNOW THE LEDGERS ARE SAFE?
JUST KNOW, IF ANYTHING HAPPENS TO ME OR BETTY, THE FEDS WILL HAVE 'EM WITHIN A DAY. NES PAS?
NES PAS.

I TRUST YOU HAVEN'T SEEN THIS, OR YOU'D KNOW YOUR FIRST REQUEST IS ALREADY TAKEN CARE OF...

San Francisco Times

MASS-MURDERER!

PERVERT PRIEST DEAD AFTER SFPD SHOOTOUT

THESE OTHER REQUESTS ARE PALTRY, I MUST SAY.
A SIMPLE MAN'S GOT SIMPLE NEEDS, THORPE.

HRMM. YOU'VE PROVEN YOU ARE ANYTHING BUT SIMPLE, MR. GRISSEL.
SAYS YOU.

WELL ALL OF THIS IS DOABLE. THOUGH THIS LAST ONE MIGHT PROVE A LITTLE TRICKY.
BUT IT'S NOTHING A HEALTHY ENDOWMENT WON'T FIX...

THORPE UNIVERSI

THORPE HALL
UNIVERSITY OF BERKELEY

SCHOO PSYCHI
MED INE

Karen Horney Self-Analysis

MISS GRISSEL?

OH, DR. RICE!
YOUR PAPER INTRIGUED ME.
"RELIGIOUS MANIA IN THE MALE HOMOSEXUAL."

RADICAL STUFF. HAVE YOU CONCLUDED YOUR RESEARCH?
YEAH, IT ENDED WITH A REAL BANG.

SEPTEMBER, 1953.
Day after day. The same thing. Until suddenly it ain't.
TODAY'S MUSIC
ODETTA
Blood of the Lamb got whitewashed away. Now it's crawling with Bohemians. Dunno which is worse.
Of course, THORPE still owns the joint.
THE TIN ANGEL CAFE
But now it ain't tax free.

Sometimes change don't show on the outside.
But inside...

... it's a whole 'nother ball game.

Loretta used to tell me the Coit Tower was the only dick in town bigger n' me.

San Francisco's got no graveyards.

Only room for the LIVING in this town.
VALENTINE MEMORIAL

And it's in the Colonel's best interests t'keep me that way.

So, he got me PROTECTION.
Some muscle of my own.

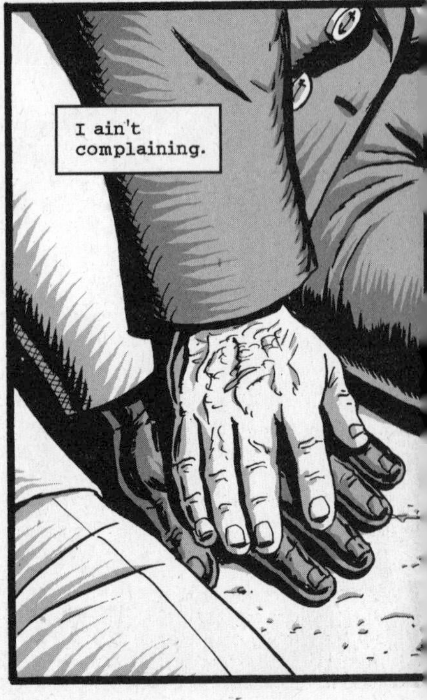
I ain't complaining.

My favorite time of day in the City--
-- After the morning fog burns off and before the evening fog rolls in--
-- And everything's so clear.
Just before it ain't again.
THE END.

MORE VERTIGO CRIME

THE CHILL
AVAILABLE NOW

Written by **JASON STARR**
(Best-selling author of *Panic Attack* and *The Follower*)

Art by **MICK BERTILORENZI**

A modern thriller steeped in Celtic mythology – a broken-down cop tracks a seductive killer who possesses the supernatural power known as "the chill." Can he stop her before her next victim dies horribly… but with a smile on his face?

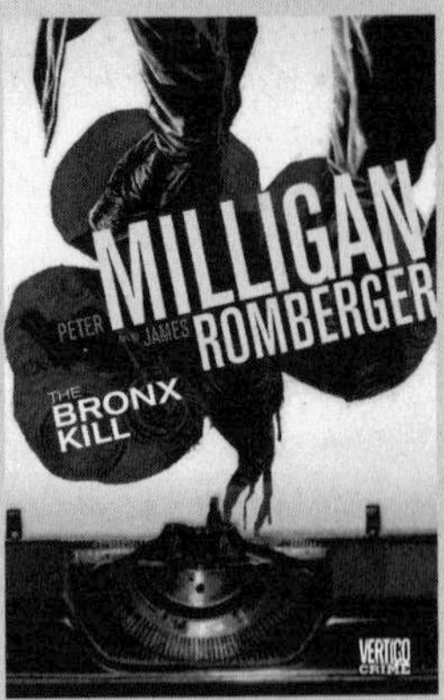

THE BRONX KILL
AVAILABLE NOW

Written by **PETER MILLIGAN**
(GREEK STREET)

Art by **JAMES ROMBERGER**

A struggling writer is investigating his Irish cop roots for his next novel. When he returns home from a research trip, his wife is missing and finding her will lead him to a dark secret buried deep in his family's past.

THE EXECUTOR
AVAILABLE NOW

Written by **JON EVANS**
(Author of *Dark Places* and *Invisible Armies*)

Art by **ANDREA MUTTI**

When a washed-up ex-hockey player is mysteriously named executor of an old girlfriend's will, he must return to the small town he left years earlier. There, he finds a deadly secret from his past that could hold the key to his girlfriend's murder… if it doesn't kill him first.